MODERN LIONEL TRAINS

Robert Schleicher

MBI

This edition first published in 2003 by MBI Publishing Company, Galtier Plaza, Suite 200, 380 Jackson Street, St. Paul, MN 55101-3885 USA

© Robert Schleicher, 2003

All rights reserved. With the exception of quoting brief passages for the purposes of review, no part of this publication may be reproduced without prior written permission from the Publisher.

The information in this book is true and complete to the best of our knowledge. All recommendations are made without any guarantee on the part of the author or Publisher, who also disclaim any liability incurred in connection with the use of this data or specific details.

We recognize that some words, model names and designations, for example, mentioned herein are the property of the trademark holder. We use them for identification purposes only. This is not an official publication.

MBI titles are also available at discounts in bulk quantity for industrial or sales-promotional use. For details write to Special Sales Manager at Motorbooks International Wholesalers & Distributors, Galtier Plaza, Suite 200, 380 Jackson Street, St. Paul, MN 55101-3885 USA.

ISBN 0-7603-1596-5

On the front cover:
Upper Right: Lionel's massive 4-6-6-4 Challenger is an articulated locomotive on which each set of drivers pivots beneath the boiler.
Lower Right: Lionel's most realistic diesel locomotive to date, the 2003 exact-scale replica o fthe Santa Fe F-3A diesel complete with marker flags and other superdetails.
Lower Left: Lionel's New York central 4-6-4 Hudson with the streamlined shrouding conceived by industrial designer Henry Dreyfuss.

On the frontispiece: During the 1990s, Lionel offered the massive Grain Elevator as one in a series of plastic building kits. The decals were not included.

On the title page: The Pennsylvania Railroad 4-8-2 Mountain-type steam locomotive is one of Lionel's most massive locomotives, with a wheelbase so long it can negotiate only 54-inch or larger curves.

On the back cover: Lionel has offered its 1860s-era 4-4-0 *General* in a variety of paint schemes, including the Virginia & Truckee livery seen here from 1988.

Edited by Dennis Pernu
Cover designed by Brian Janni
Interior designed by Mandy Iverson

Printed in China

CONTENTS

INTRODUCTION		6
CHAPTER 1	**The Transition Era of Lionel Toy Trains**	10
CHAPTER 2	**Lionel Comes Back**	18
CHAPTER 3	**Lionel Comes Back, Bigger Than Ever**	32
CHAPTER 4	**Lionel on Their Own Again**	52
CHAPTER 5	**The Lionel Dream Fulfilled**	74
INDEX		94

INTRODUCTION

Lionel's exact-scale Harriman 2-8-0 and an extruded-aluminum Union Pacific passenger train rumble through a town assembled from Lione's plastic kits of the 1990s.

Mom, apple pie, and Lionel trains are some of the things that Americans consider secure. Hula hoops, Hush Puppies, white sidewall tires, and even Beanie Babies have come and gone, but Lionel trains remain. In truth, Lionel is a stronger and better product line today than at any time since the 1940s and 1950s.

The Lionel locomotives, cars, and accessories you see on these pages represent the changeover from post–World War II standards of quality and production to twenty-first-century standards of excellence, and the shift from being 10 percent "Made in America" to being entirely "Made in China." Lionel, however, is still very much an American company, with the design and engineering and marketing departments in Michigan, USA.

This Is the Golden Age of Lionel

Like many classic toys, the Lionel you buy today may seem like the Lionel you remember from 40 or 50 years ago, but guess what? Your memories are rose-colored. Those older Lionel trains are no matches for the products you can buy today. Our expectations of quality, detail, finish, authenticity, and performance have risen exponentially in just the past decade or so, and Lionel has kept pace with those demands. You can still buy "mint in box" (and some not quite so pristine examples that you'd actually dare to take out of the box and run) Lionel products from the early postwar years. Few of them, though, run as well as the newest Lionel products and none have the same level of detail as today's Lionel.

The skilled but incredibly low-cost labor available in Asia has completely changed the toy industry. From the 1950s through even the 1980s, a hobby product was expected to have far more detail and realism than a toy. It simply cost too much to include the same amount of detail in a toy. And, anyway, who would care? It was a toy. When American and European manufacturers first began to use Asian manufacturers, they did so purely because of cost. But as manufacturing skills improved in Asia, American and European companies found the quality of the products could be improved.

Not all toy makers took that route; some of them continued to make cheap toys. Some, including giants like Mattel, wanted to increase quality while keeping prices about the same. Asia responded to the challenge to produce, for example, the thousands of different diecast trucks and automobiles (with incredible detail, exact scale, and perfect trim and lettering) that today flood chain stores like Wal-Mart and Target.

If you're willing to wait or search, you can buy anything Lionel ever made. I've listed some of the highlights of Lionel's production for each decade, but remember: Lionel usually reintroduces virtually all of their locomotives, cars, and accessories after a few years, so you will likely eventually find out-of-production items if you are patient. If you are impatient, try eBay or the swap meets listed in *Classic Toy Trains* magazine.

Hobby Quality at Toy Prices

Today, Lionel occupies a rather unique position in the toy business. They have always produced toys that are expensive enough to qualify them (in most folks' minds) as "hobby" items rather than just throwaway toys. Lionel also makes a line of relatively inexpensive O-27 trains sets and products, but even those are far too rugged and reliable to relegate to the trash like you might have with a Tyco HO train set.

As hobby manufacturers discovered that Asian manufacturers could make products as good as or better than those made in America, Lionel decided to try production outside the United States. Actually, the company turned to Mexico first, in the mid-1980s, and nearly went bankrupt due to a lack of consistent quality. Lionel next turned to Korea,

Even exact-scale Lionel equipment can operate on tight 31-inch or 42-inch circles of track set up around the Christmas tree.

Lionel's "superdetailed" F-3A and F-3B diesels from 2003 are exact O scale replicas.

which had become the world's largest producer of model railroad locomotives fabricated from brass. In the 1980s, Lionel found a Korean maker that was just beginning to learn how to produce cast-metal products in addition to hand-crafted brass, and the Lionel Standard O line of rolling stock and exact-scale locomotives was reborn, resurrecting a series that had started before World War II.

Until 2001, when all of Lionel's production was moved to China, Lionel continued to use their Mount Clemens, Michigan, factory in suburban Detroit to produce their O-27 and smaller O Gauge locomotives, cars, accessories, and track that had been first introduced in the 1950s and 1960s. The vast majority of the tooling to produce those products had been amortized decades ago, so the only real cost was labor and maintenance of the tooling. When new dies and tooling needed to be produced, however, it was too costly to do so in America. Lionel introduced one or two

All Lionel's O, O-27, and Standard O equipment can operate on Lionel's three-rail track.

Lionel crossing gates and semaphores are inexpensive mechanical operating accessories. The Crossing Gateman's Shanty seen here is Lione's most famous operating accessory.

new items a year, but 95 percent of the line was simply new paint jobs on old products. Today, Lionel regularly introduces a dozen or more new products every year, more than at any other time in their history.

This book is not intended to be collecting or price guide. Several of those are available from most shops that sell Lionel. My intention is to provide a broad overview of the products Lionel has made of over the past 30-odd years so you can search out stuff you did not know existed, or simply better appreciate what you have accumulated so far.

Aesthetically speaking, Lionel trains are perhaps the most impressive model trains ever made. They are massive, yet small enough so you can actually see most of an entire train on a shelf. Lionel trains are even more fun to run for the simple reason that they run reliably, with no need for labyrinthine wiring and control levers, and with a floor-shaking rumble and presence that is as realistic as the shape and color of the trains themselves. To most model railroaders and toy-train collectors, Lionel trains are the most real of all the miniature trains.

Lionel's exact-scale New York Central Railroad Henry "Dreyfuss"–shrouded 4-6-4 Hudson has been available in two different road numbers from Lionel.

CHAPTER 1
The Transition Era of Lionel Toy Trains

Lionel offers bridges and bridge abutments to allow two-level or over-and-under figure-8 layouts.

Fond Memories of Toy Trains or Real Railroads?

The desire to have miniature trains may be rooted in our memories. There seems to be something almost genetic about our fascination with trains. What is it about watching one car trail so perfectly after another that appeals to most folks, even if it's a baggage train on rubber tires at an airport? For some of us the sight of that first toy train is never forgotten and the desire to have one or more is hard to satisfy completely. For others, it's the memory of real trains that mesmerizes us and drives us to want miniature re-creations of that experience.

Lionel offers products for both type of fan. For those who prefer to relive "toy" train experiences, Lionel always has new items in their O-27 series, and O Gauge trains with a variety of Christmastime and other fantasy decorations, toy airplanes, and a host of other toy delights. For those who prefer to have real railroads, just smaller, Lionel offers Standard O replicas that are accurate down to the scale inch, and a range of "semi-scale" O Gauge trains that are also very realistic. Most of us like 'em all.

A Lionel Gauge Primer

Lionel is generally referred to as "O Gauge," which is true: the spacing between the rails is very close to a scale 4 feet, 8-1/2 inches (about 1-3/16 inches when reduced to O Gauge's 1/48 scale). The size of the models that run on that track varies, however.

Lionel produces three distinct product lines: O-27, O Gauge, and Standard O (or, more simply, "Standard"). All three will run on the same track, although Standard O cars and exact-scale "O scale" locomotives require much larger curves of up to 72 inches in circumference. The O-27 trains are the least expensive Lionel products and O-27 track is about half the weight of O scale track, though the curved route through the O-27 switches is a bit sharp for some of the O scale locomotives.

Lionel products represent equipment from all eras of real railroading, including the 1860-era *General* 4-4-0 with both freight and passenger cars from 1988.

True O scale is 1/48 scale, or 1/4 inch to the foot. Lionel O-27 cars and locomotives are usually not true O scale, but rather closer to 1/64 or S scale, the size of American Flyer's toy trains (which Lionel also reproduces from time to time). O Gauge Lionel trains are nearer to 1/48 scale, but most are somewhat shorter and narrower than exact scale. Standard O cars and larger locomotives are accurate 1/48-scale reproductions.

In short, Lionel has a seemingly random method of selecting scales. While the O-27 Alco FA-1 is tiny, barely 1/64 scale, the O-27 GP7 diesel and Alco RS3 are very close to correct 1/48 scale. The Lionel O-27 hopper, meanwhile, is 2 inches wide, their O Gauge 40-foot boxcars are 2-1/4 inches wide, and the Standard-O boxcars are 2-1/2 inches wide. To put this in perspective, most full-size freight cars are about 10 feet wide, which reduces to 2-1/2 inches in 1/48 scale (1-7/8 inches in 1/64 scale). But, somehow, this variance really doesn't seem to matter: The cars and locomotives look just fine.

If the odd mixture of proportions bothers you, stick to using Lionel O Gauge or Standard O and you should be satisfied. Actually, many feel that a true-length passenger car looks out of place on a Lionel layout anyway, even on 72-inch curved track (the broadest curve circumference sold by Lionel). The slightly shortened "Madison" series of heavyweight-style cars, the extruded-aluminum "corrugated" cars, and the aluminum smooth-side passenger cars like the Union Pacific dome cars in this book, for example, are all about a scale 60 feet long—nearly 20 percent too short. Still, they look good on any Lionel layout. Conversely, the Lionel O-27 Alco FA-1 and EMD FT diesels and the O-27 streamlined passenger cars are so short they look toylike. But, then again, they *are* toys.

Introduced in 1992, the three-truck Western Maryland Shay locomotive was one of Lionel's first exact O scale steam locomotives. It has been offered in several road names.

Larger Lionel Trains

Lionel also makes limited-edition reproductions of older Lionel tin-toy O Gauge and Standard O trains originally produced in the 1930s, Large Scale (G scale) trains that can be run in the garden, and occasional limited reproductions of American Flyer S Gauge cars, locomotives, and accessories.

If you are not confused yet, consider that Lionel occasionally offers stamped-metal reproductions, and some new creations, in what they call "Standard Gauge." This model size dates from the first half of the twentieth century and was used by Lionel and others for stamped-steel "tinplate" toy trains. The distance, or gauge, between Standard Gauge rails is 2-1/8 inches. Large Scale (also called "G scale") track and trains, also offered by Lionel, are actually smaller than Standard Gauge, at 1-3/4 inches between the rails.

OK, one more thing: On real railroads, "Standard Gauge" is just that: the track gauge used by every mainline railroad in America.

Hi-Rail

The rail on all Lionel track is about five times larger than exact scale. Why? Because cars and locomotives with large wheel flanges stay on the track even when that track is laid on a floor as uneven as one covered with shag carpet. That third rail and the oversize rails are much of the reason why Lionel trains and tracks are so reliable.

This sampling of the locomotives Lionel offered in late 2002 and early 2003 is displayed on the "Wall of Trains" at Mizell Trains in Westminster, Colorado.

Lionel's O-27, O Gauge, and Standard O trains are near enough in size to operate together without looking out of place.

Serious O scale model railroaders use two rails, however, because they prefer the realism to the simplicity of wiring offered by Lionel's three-rail track with non-scale rails. These modelers also prefer the much smaller rail that is proportionally scaled to real railroad rail. Lionel does offer some of their accurately scaled Standard O locomotives with smaller flanges on the drivers and wheels for those who want to operate on this scale-size rail.

Model railroaders who want the best of both the exact-scale world and the three-rail world use three-rail track with exact-scale locomotives and rolling stock. These locomotives and cars built to exact O scale to operate on three-rail track are referred to as "Hi-rail" because of the proportionally too-high size of the rail. During the past decade or so, Lionel has offered several new accurate O scale products each year. O scale Hi-rail cars and locomotives are also available from Lionel's major competitors, MTH and K-Line, as well as Atlas, Weaver, Williams, and others.

Retiring on the Value of Your Lionel Collection
The real value in Lionel trains lies in their "play value," which can mean the pleasure of watching them run, the pleasure of just looking at them, or both. In a very few cases, folks have made a profit by buying and selling older Lionel trains, but today profit is rare.

Yes, a Lionel Hudson that sold for $100 in 1940 might bring $3,000 or more today, but that does not begin to cover the cost of inflation. You'd have made many times that profit over five decades by just leaving your money in a savings account at a bank. Generally, the price of a "mint" collector's item is about the same as a similar product bought new. The very, very few Lionel items that are valuable are very limited-production items that are perhaps a different color or that feature different decorations. Most out-of-production Lionel products actually sell for less than their current counterparts. These trains are designed for your viewing and operating pleasure, not to provide for a future retirement or to pay for your kid's education.

There is no way to set a price on the value Lionel trains provide each of us. Lionel trains are memories brought to life, memories you can hold in your hand, watch in motion. The Lionel trains you can buy today are more than just nostalgia. They are better than nostalgia because they are not rusty and faded antiques, but brand-new re-creations of both original Lionel toys and real railroad locomotives and cars that run reliably and rumble and roar across the floor or tabletop, just as we always dreamed they would.

The Lionel FB-1 (left) and FA-1 became the diesels included in most of Lionel's entry-level train sets in the 1940s. Ralph Johnson's F-3A (right) in Wabash colors is actually a rare one from 1955.

CHAPTER 2
Lionel Comes Back

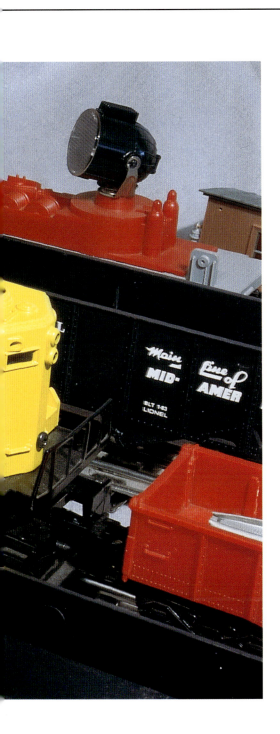

Lionel's EMD GP7 has been offered in more than a dozen different paint schemes, including the Chicago & North Western "Route of the Streamliners" livery seen here from 1983.

Ralph Johnson created this permanent Lionel layout from 1x4 and 2x4 lumber with plaster scenery.

Lionel came every close to disappearing in the early 1970s. The Lionel Corporation began back in 1918 and survived World War II to enter the plastic age. For whatever reason, however, Lionel lost its market and plummeted from being the world's largest toy maker in about 1950 to being nearly worthless by 1964. Hobbyists and collectors will long debate the "why?" of Lionel's near demise. Some say folks simply defected to HO scale; others feel it was just ineffective management. Whatever the case, in 1969 Lionel was for sale.

That year, the management of General Mills' hobby division, MPC, felt it was worth the gamble and purchased Lionel. They relocated the company from New York City to Mount Clemens, Michigan, and later moved Lionel into their Fundimensions Division to be marketed alongside their Craftmaster paint-by-numbers kits and the MPC plastic model car and truck kits. The original Lionel Corporation continued as a marketing firm with the Kiddie City chain of toy stores and other endeavors until it went bankrupt in 1995.

Lionel Toy Trains

Lionel's MPC/Fundimensions era was a period when Lionel produced some of the least expensive products in their history in the hope of retaining a market share with mass merchandisers like K-Mart and Toys R Us. Ultimately, those marketplaces voted for $30 train sets over $300 train sets and Lionel lost nearly all of its mass-market shelf space to the much less expensive HO trains. The Fundimensions folks fought even harder to reestablish Lionel's hobby market. They understood the "collector" concept and began to feature cars, locomotives, and sets with more limited-production decorations in Lionel catalogs.

Fundimensions continued the Lionel program of producing new products from tooling that had been created in the 1950s. Every year or so, another piece of original postwar-era tooling was resurrected, refurbished, and put

Ralph Johnson could not wait for Lionel's *Texas Special*, which was introduced in 1999, so he repainted his set of extruded-aluminum corrugated passenger cars. The diesels are Lionel's Baltimore & Ohio F-3A and F-3B units.

Lionel offered plastic building kits throughout most of the 1970s, including this example that they simply called Freight Station.

The Lionel Searchlight Car has always been a favorite, providing quite a dramatic sight as it flashes its beam while the train pulls it around the track in a darkened room.

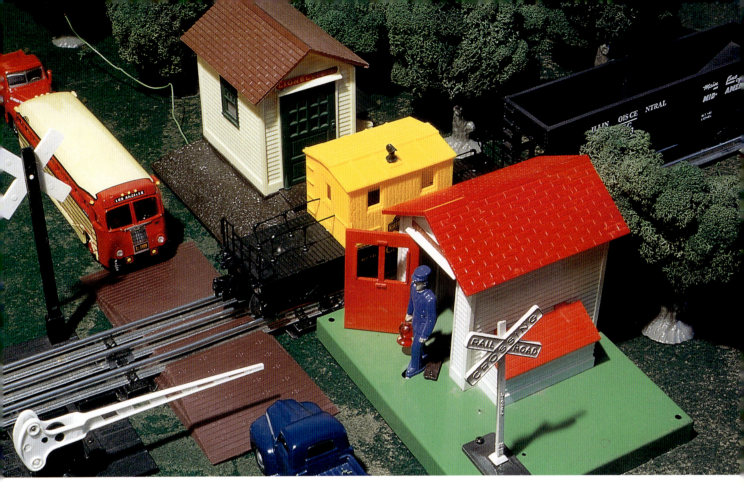

In the 1970s, Lionel offered an operating Gateman's Shanty, as well as a pair of structures to house an operating diesel horn and a steam locomotive whistle.

into production. As Lionel struggled just to stay alive, very little new tooling was created from 1962 to 1972. It took a few years, but Fundimensions finally reawakened the market for Lionel trains enough for the company to afford new tooling.

The 1970s were a simple time for the Lionel enthusiast. The relatively expensive remote-controlled coal- and log loaders and other operating accessories were only available as collector pieces from the 1950s. Also during the 1970s, hobbyists were excited about building models from kits; the era of the ready-built was still decades away. The plastic building kits that Lionel introduced in that decade probably did add to the appeal of their products. The buildings certainly offered items that had not ever been available from Lionel. Interestingly, Lionel called their ready-built station a "Passenger Station" and the kit a "Freight Station," even though there was also a kit for the "Freight Platform."

Lionel's 2-4-2 diesel has been used as a locomotive in their inexpensive train sets, as the power for ballast tampers, and as this Union Pacific rotary snowplow from 2001.

Lionel has offered EMD's EP5 electric locomotive in several real railroad paint schemes, including the New Haven's famous McGinnis livery. The metal pantographs on the roof do not carry current.

The 1970s also saw the introduction of inexpensive crossing gates and semaphore signals that were actuated by the weight of the train passing over a spring trigger. No lighting was provided with these mechanical accessories. Fundimensions also used their skills in molding plastic to produce a kit that loaded coal mechanically and, later, a mechanical log loader.

New Products for the 1970s

Lionel began to create new tooling in the early 1970s. In 1973, the mold for their Electro-Motive (EMD) GP7 and GP9 was modified to produce an alternate "low-nose" that Lionel called a GP20. The following year, Lionel produced their first all-new diesel in nearly two decades, the General Electric U36B, and in 1978 rolled out their first "Modern Era" six-axle diesels by fitting six-wheel trucks beneath the GP20 to produce the SD18. In 1979 Lionel also fitted the trucks to the U36B to produce a U36C. The locomotives weren't popping out a dozen a year like they would in the 1990s, but it was enough to get the attention of current and prospective Lionel fans, alike.

In the 1970s, Lionel also produced some new freight cars, starting in 1973 with an O scale 40-foot boxcar, a 40-foot plug-door reefer, and a three-deck auto rack that Lionel called an "Auto Carrier." The boxcar was fitted with spring trucks and prefigured Lionel's reentry into the O scale market in 1986.

In 1972 Lionel also produced their least-expensive train set, the 0-4-0T locomotive, accompanied by a four-wheel boxcar and a gondola of no known prototype and a four-wheel caboose that was similar to many American cabooses from the turn of the twentieth century.

Lionel also produced a smaller version of their classic 1937 New York Central Hudson 4-6-4 steam locomotive in 1972, complete with "Sound of Steam" and whistle. An improved version with MagneTraction was introduced in 1976 and Lionel later offered the locomotive in a variety of paint schemes, including the New York Central, Chesapeake & Ohio, New Jersey Central, and, in 1979, Santa Fe. The Santa Fe 4-6-4 was part of the first "Famous American Railroad Series," a set without track that included the locomotive with freight cars painted for one railroad, in this case the Santa Fe.

Also in 1979, Lionel introduced a new series of "long" streamlined passenger cars constructed with extruded-aluminum bodies and plastic ends. The first set of these 15-inch-long cars was made of polished aluminum to re-create the Pennsylvania Railroad's *Congressional Limited* train with its corrugated sides and ends.

Lionel began to market some remote-control operating accessories in the early 1970s. They introduced a pair of "sound" buildings, one that emitted the sound of a diesel horn and the other the sound of steam locomotive whistle, at the touch of a button. Both used a shed similar to the Lionel's classic Automatic Gateman's Shanty. In 1975 Lionel introduced an operating drawbridge.

Lionel's version of the NW 2 switcher diesel has been made available in a variety of paint schemes, including this "zebra-striped" Santa Fe model from the late 1990s.

Lionel's 75th Anniversary

For Lionel's 75th anniversary in 1975, Fundimensions (labeled as "A Division of General Mills Fun Group, Inc.") unveiled a series of plastic structure kits to increase the "play value" of Lionel trains at a minimum cost to the consumer. A passenger station, freight platform, water tower, and engine house were the first four kits. The classic operating gateman, automatic crossing gates, and working signals were the only operating accessories offered in the 1970s—the reintroduction of operating accessories like the 1950s-era log loaders and coal loaders would have to wait for the 1980s.

The 75th anniversary Lionel catalog had just 48 pages (compared to the 1950 catalog with 50 pages and the two 2003 catalogs with a total of 220 pages). The only "new" locomotive was the reintroduced EP5 electric that Lionel incorrectly called a "Little Joe," manufactured from postwar-era tooling and offered in a Pennsylvania Railroad paint scheme, followed up with Great Northern and Milwaukee models in 1976 and 1977. Lionel reintroduced the postwar General Electric E-33 electric locomotive in 1976 and the famous GG1 electric in 1977.

The locomotive lineup for 1975 was typical of the decade and included the O-27 FA-1 and FB-1, and the O Gauge GP7 and GP9, NW2, U36B, EP5, and F3A in several paint schemes for a total of 18 models. There were also three O-27 steam locomotives: the 0-4-0T tank engine with no tender, the 0-4-0 switcher, and the traditional 2-4-2 train set. A small O Gauge 4-6-4 Hudson was Lionel's "top of the line" locomotive.

The Madison series of heavyweight passenger cars has been part of the Lionel line since the 1940s. The cars were reintroduced in the 1970s; this is one of the later examples with an observation platform.

The Lionel Operating Boxcar has appeared in dozens of paint schemes over the years. It unloads barrels, crates, and mailbags by remote control.

Lionel's postwar-era operating milk car was reintroduced with a larger body in 1983.

In the 1970s, Lionel offered both the NW2 switcher and the "train set" 2-4-2, like those in Ralph Johnson's layout.

Lionel offered just two passenger cars in 1975, an O-27 heavyweight Pullman and combine in either Pennsy maroon or Milwaukee orange.

Lionel offered a total of four operating freight cars in the 1970s: a post-office boxcar (from which a workman pushed bags, barrels, or boxes out the door), a searchlight car, a log car, and a coal car. All were activated when a small metal disc on a lever beneath the car was attracted by the electromagnet in the Remote Control Operating Track section. A similar disc was used with the track section to activate the uncoupling mechanism for the automatic couplers.

Lionel's most significant achievement of the 1970s, however, was that it not only survived but it began to grow and could, after decades of doldrums, begin to afford new tooling for its locomotives, cars, and accessories.

Lionel introduced their series of 15-inch-long, extruded-aluminum, smooth-side passenger cars in 1983.

CHAPTER 3
Lionel Comes Back, Bigger Than Ever

The 1980s became the most exciting time in Lionel's history since the 1950s. Fundimensions made excellent progress throughout the first half of the decade. The new tooling purchased in the late 1970s was beginning to pay off—soon the new products were generating enough profits to invest in more new tooling. Lionel had barely survived the 1960s and 1970s by refurbishing their existing dies, made back in the 1950s. The initial tooling investment in the late 1970s was small enough to at least make it a potentially profitable venture.

Enthusiasts like to believe that the success of Lionel in the 1990s and today is the result of Richard Kughn, but he did not arrive until 1986. Certainly, a lot of the products that helped resurrect Lionel appeared in the late 1980s, but

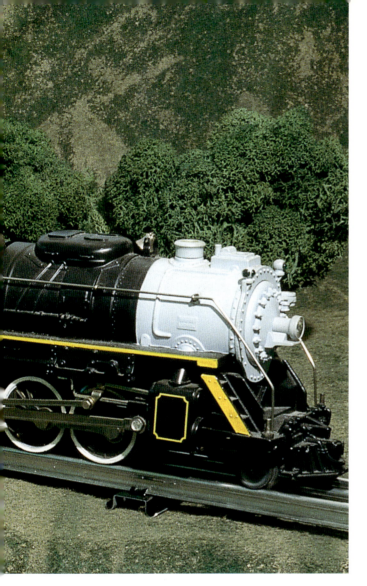

The Lionel O Gauge 2-8-4 has been one of the most popular medium-size steam locomotives for decades. This is a 1970s version in Chesapeake & Ohio paint and lettering.

The Richard J. Kughn Era, 1986–96

Richard J. Kughn was an enthusiast and collector with enough wealth to amass one of the country's largest toy train collections. When he heard that General Mills might be willing to divest itself of what the cereal giant still considered a struggling division not producing the sort of volume or profit desired, he bought it all. For the first time since Joshua Lionel Cohen died in 1969, Lionel's "captain" was a toy train enthusiast. Lionel was truly reborn.

Richard Kughn gave Lionel both the freedom to expand and the money to do so. And as Lionel rose to the challenge with more and better new products, the American public responded by purchasing all that Lionel could make.

An Abundance of Products

In the 1980s, Lionel expanded into just about every known model railroad area except N and HO scales. Presumably, Lionel management figured that, while there were already too many manufacturers of HO and N scale models, there was still a market for more S scale, G gauge, and Standard Gauge models. It was a period of growth in new products that exceeded even the golden era of the 1950s. In addition, Lionel reintroduced postwar-era items and, at the end of the 1980s, O scale products.

given design, tooling, and production lead times, most of those products were brought into being before Kughn arrived. Whatever the case, Kughn certainly helped provide the funding that allowed the designs to reach the production stage, and in the process led Lionel back to the prominence it had enjoyed in the postwar period.

Lionel in the 1980s found themselves in a market that was about one-tenth the size of their market in the 1950s. In the 1950s, model trains were among the most popular leisure-time activities available. By the 1980s, there were literally thousands of ways to spend disposable money and time. Still, the market was large enough for Lionel to

Lionel has offered its 1860-era 4-4-0 *General* in a variety of paint schemes, including the Virginia & Truckee livery seen here in 1988.

amortize the tooling for new products of all kinds. There were still more than enough grandparents and parents who remembered the trains they had wanted in their youth, and Lionel was there to fulfill those dreams, regardless of what they might be.

Helping Lionel was the fact that nostalgia was beginning to sweep America. Everything from old Coca-Cola bottles to Barbie dolls became icons. At least two generations of Americans had reached an age where they had both disposal income and an interest in the toys they wanted but could not afford as children or as young parents.

Lionel tried every marketing and cross-marketing idea they could. They produced a board game called "Double Crossing" in 1988 that was, essentially, a railroad version of "Monopoly," where players assembled both a train and an empire. The pencil-sized trains lent a toy train atmosphere and the game was at least as much fun as the board game "Sorry".

Lionel even published its own book, *The Lionel Train Book*, in 1986, the first book they had published since *The Handbook for Model Builders* in 1941.

American Flyer versus Lionel

In the 1950s, American Flyer and Lionel were major competitors. Lionel had the massive size of O Gauge and the simplicity of three-rail on their side. American Flyer, on the other hand, offered more precise scale and realism of just two rails. Those who grew up in that era seem to be enthusiastic fans of either one or the other, but seldom are they fans of both brands.

The American Flyer tooling was available at bargain-basement prices, so it made sense for Lionel to control all of the "larger" toy train market. It was a risk, then, for Lionel to reintroduce the American Flyer brand in the mid-1980s, and even more of a risk to include American Flyer in their catalogs. But it worked. With American Flyer manufactured by Lionel, the old split seemed to be healed. Lionel even produced an American Flyer set as the fifth in their 1980s "Famous American Railroad Series," a Southern Pacific train with a GP9, boxcar, flatcar with trailers, three-dome tank car, hopper, gondola with containers, and caboose for 1987.

The "Collector Series" catalog for 1986 devoted five of its 16 pages to American Flyer products, including two complete freight trains (as individual pieces, not sets).

The rift between Lionel and American Flyer fans is still not completely healed, however; few books and price guides on Lionel products for the 1980–2003 period include American Flyer. Even the operating accessories, which are often more exciting than Lionel's own reproductions, are not in the guides. (And there have been some great American Flyer operating accessories, although not all have been identified as coming from American Flyer tooling

Lionel introduced shorter versions of their heavyweight, Madison-style passenger cars in the 1980s in several prototype liveries.

Lionel's Large Scale 4-4-2 was an accurate 1/32 scale replica of a Santa Fe locomotive. Large Scale trains run on two-rail track.

and designs, including the Oil Drum Loader introduced in the late 1980s and the Seaboard Coaler introduced in 2002.) If you want to know about American Flyer, even those products made by Lionel, you need to look at an American Flyer price guide.

Direct Sales

In the 1980s, Lionel tried everything that management could imagine to bring the company forward. In 1986, however, they went a step too far when they produced a special run of the Standard O semi-scale Hudson 4-6-4 steam locomotives, painted and lettered for the Boston & Albany Railroad, and introduced the scale New York Central caboose.

The locomotive, along with a matching B&A caboose, the NYC caboose, and five other freight cars were offered for sale only direct to consumers. None of these items were available from hobby dealers, which understandably created a dealer revolt that almost killed Lionel. Fortunately, around this time, Richard Kughn bought the company and helped soothe the dealers' frustrations. Direct-sale-only items were not attempted again.

Large Scale

There is a popular model railroad and toy train size even larger than Standard Gauge called, appropriately, Large Scale. Large Scale trains were pioneered by LGB in Germany in the late 1960s as models of European narrow gauge locomotives and cars. The LGB models operated on track of a 1-3/4-inch gauge, which, on scale, was close to the 1-meter gauge commonly used for most European narrow gauge trains, and close to the 3-foot gauge that was most common for American narrow gauge trains. When the scale of the LGB trains was matched to the size of the track, G scale became 1/22.5 scale, which resulted in models that are even larger than the Standard Gauge reproductions of 1930s-era toys.

Lionel entered the G scale market in 1987 with the 0-6-0T old-time locomotive, a short eight-wheeled, simulated-wood gondola, flatcar, and caboose. All of the equipment was based on shortened American narrow

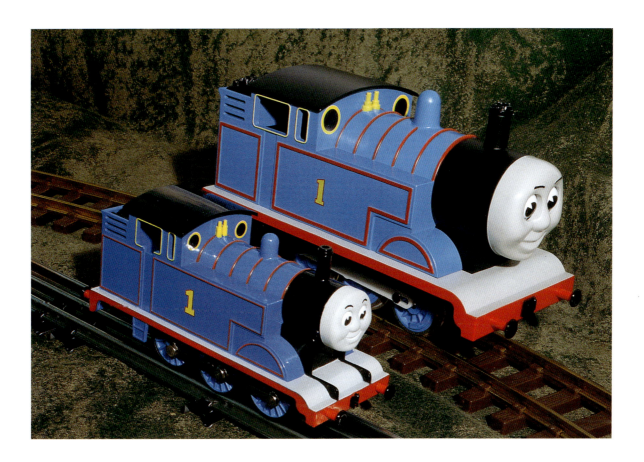

Lionel produces both Large Scale and O scale re-creations of "Thomas the Tank Engine."

gauge prototypes and built to about the same 1/22.5 scale as LGB trains. Lionel produced its own track with hollow rail similar to O Gauge track but with brass rail and plastic ties. Unlike the LGB track, which was designed for the "garden railroad" hobby, Lionel's could not be left permanently outdoors.

Then, Lionel started its own version of Large Scale in 1989 with the introduction of a series of models of Standard Gauge locomotives and cars to run on G gauge track. These new models were about 1/32 scale, which made them similar in size to 1/22.5 scale narrow gauge cars and locomotives. The first Lionel Large Scale Standard Gauge locomotive was the Pennsylvania Railroad 4-4-2 Atlantic. These models operate on the G gauge track from Lionel, LGB, Aristo-Craft, Bachmann, USA Trains, and others. The Atlantic, however, is very close to 1/32 scale, which would be the correct size for that 1-3/4-inch track. In fact, the models are a resurrection of a scale that Lionel and others produced in the 1930s called "1 Gauge," which was 1/32 scale equipment (give or take—they were tinplate toys, after all) operating on track with 1-3/4-inch gauge.

In 1988, Lionel expanded the Large Scale line with a more modern eight-wheeled boxcar, a plug-door reefer, and a very toy-like passenger coach. In 1989, Lionel added a working handcar, an eight-wheeled tank car, an ore car, a searchlight car, and a four-wheel caboose to the line. The proportions of these models were more like those of the 4-4-2 Atlantic. Lionel only produced one more piece of 1/32 scale equipment, a series of similar GP7 and GP9, GP20 diesels, all based on a common set of production tooling, beginning in 1990.

Lionel reintroduced the Fairbanks-Morse TrainMaster diesel in the mid-1980s. This is a 2002 version.

The cab on Lionel's Magnetic Crane rotates, its boom goes up and down, the cable raises and lowers the hook, and the magnet can be actuated to lift steel rails.

Even though the Large Scale trains were not designed for outdoor use, Lionel introduced a series of all-wood building kits that could be used outdoors. The line included a passenger station, water tower, watchman's shanty, lumberyard, freight platform, and a single-stall engine house.

Thomas the Tank, Full-Size

The locomotives and rolling stock used to film the television series *Thomas & Friends* are very close to G gauge. In 1989, Lionel took advantage of the Large Scale tooling to offer a replica of the famous Thomas the Tank Engine locomotive. The kids didn't know it, but Lionel's model of Thomas was very close indeed to the size of the "real" Thomas used to film the scenes for television series and the motion picture.

Onboard Television with Railscope

Lionel tried a wide range of products in the 1980s in an effort to make toy trains interesting to more people than just collectors. One of the most interesting of these efforts was an onboard television camera. Lionel called the system Railscope when it was introduced in 1988, and it was only produced until 1990. The system included a special video camera mounted inside the locomotive with the camera

The Pennsylvania Railroad S-2 6-8-6 steam turbine was one of Lionel's most popular locomotives in the mid-1940s. It was reintroduced in the mid-1980s as part of the Famous American Railroad series.

Throughout most of the 1980s, Lionel offered sets of cars (like this Pennsylvania Railroad tankcar) painted to match railroads in the Famous American Railroad series.

A caboose was one of the car types included in the Famous American Railroad series.

lens replacing the headlight of the locomotive to maintain realism. The camera was powered by a battery but the signal was sent through the rails either to the operator's video receiver or to a 4-1/2-inch video screen from Lionel. The picture was black and white, but quite clear. Battery life was relatively short, but there was certainly enough power for several tours of even a large layout. The major drawback to the unit was the model railroad itself—if the layout had superb scenery, that's what you saw; if the "layout" was the living room floor, you saw a lot of chair and table legs.

The concept is fascinating but most fans want to see the trains, not what the trains see. The system was offered in special gray-and-blue GP9 diesel for O and O-27, and in a Large Scale 0-4-0T. It was even available in a pair of FA2 diesels in HO scale.

Made in America

The 1980s were the beginning of nearly two decades of steady growth for Lionel trains, mostly produced in Mount Clemens, Michigan. It was certainly a challenge to produce large diesels and large steam locomotives made with all-new tooling, but Lionel designers and production staff rose to the challenge and produced more new tooling from 1980 to 1989 than they did during their heyday in the 1950s.

The truly classic postwar Lionel New York Central 4-6-4 Hudson steam locomotive and the EMD F-3A and F-3B diesels were re-created with completely new bodies and chassis that exceeded the performance and the appearance of the original models. Lionel also managed to crank out new versions of other postwar icons such as the Pennsylvania Railroad 6-8-6 Turbine steam locomotive, the 2-8-4 Berkshire steam locomotive, and the Fairbanks-Morse TrainMaster 12-wheeled diesel. At the end of the 1980s, Lionel produced the first of what would be an ongoing series of true O scale locomotives, the massive 4-8-4 Reading Railroad T-1.

Lionel also introduced more operating accessories with new dies to re-create the classic operating milk car and horse car, and the magnetic crane. The magnetic crane had been a favorite since its introduction in the 1940s, but it had been missing from the line for more than a decade. The new crane was a reproduction of the catalog No. 282 Gantry Crane built from 1954 to 1957, and was designed to roll on single rails (never supplied) like a prototype gantry crane. The original Lionel magnetic crane from the 1940s rested on a platform of a similar height. Lionel also reproduced the No. 464 Lumber Mill from the 1956 to 1960 period, and later in the decade introduced the 352 Animated Ice Depot that originally was made from 1955 to 1957, plus the matching reefer to accept clear plastic "ice" through a hatch in the roof.

The introduction of a few operating accessories in the late 1980s began a whole stream of reintroductions that would, over the next decade, include nearly every locomotive and every operating accessory Lionel had ever produced. It was also a promise that here was a new Lionel, one that would not only honor but also re-create its heritage.

During the 1970s, Lionel offered a series of larger plastic building kits made by Pola, including this Rico station. This model has been cut into two buildings, a passenger station and a freight station.

Throughout the 1980s, Lionel also continued its Famous American Railroad Series that it introduced in 1979 and which comprised a train set with no track. The cars and locomotives were available individually, as well as in a set, with each car in the set matching the same prototype railroad as the locomotive. The series provided an opportunity for Lionel to reintroduce, for example, the famous Pennsylvania Railroad Class S-2 6-8-6 steam turbine that was the hit of the 1946 line. This new S-2, however, was a replica of the most realistic of the O-27 models, with a Pennsylvania-prototype tender, painted dark green and featuring outside valve gear. The set included matching Pennsylvania Railroad double-door and single-door boxcars, covered hopper, tank car, and caboose.

The Fundimensions Heritage

In the late 1980s, Lionel came to realize that Fundimensions had contributed to the company's growth by beginning the production of all-new products, as opposed to reproductions of postwar models. Fundimensions had also proven that there was market for plastic structure kits, so Lionel contracted with one of the world's largest plastic model-building kit makers, Pola, to produce a series of O scale plastic structures.

Pola came out with a line that included a replica of the narrow gauge Rio Grande Railroad's station at Rico, Colorado, a coaling tower, a grain elevator, brick industrial buildings, and other structures. By the late 1990s, Lionel was producing a fully assembled, stamped-aluminum replica of the Rico station.

Made in Mexico

Toy trains do not lend themselves to mass production, especially not the kind of detailed trains produced by Lionel. Yes, Lionel was one of the first toy makers to use injection-molded plastic after World War II, but each locomotive, each car, and each piece of track required a lot of hands-on assembly time, even with jigs to make it easier.

Lionel management began to see the difficulty of selling products that were, in many cases, made by hand at mass-produced prices. Lionel's first attempt at reducing the labor portion of the cost package was to try production in Mexico in 1983. Track was the first item to be produced in the contracted Mexican plant, but quality-control problems were never solved. After investing far too much in the venture, Lionel withdrew from Mexico in 1986. By the late 1980s, some of the larger Lionel O scale locomotives were being made in Korea. The majority of Lionel's production in the 1980s, however, remained in Mount Clemens.

Tinplate Classics

During the first four decades of the twentieth century, toy trains were nearly all produced from steel sheets stamped to produce the forms of steam locomotives, freight cars, passenger cars, bridges, and accessories. O Gauge was the smallest popular size during this period, but even larger trains called "Standard Gauge" also occupied a large portion of the market.

Standard Gauge trains ran on three-rail track with spacing of 2-1/8 inches between the insides of the outer rails. (O Gauge is 1-3/16 inches between the outer rails.)

Lionel reproduced its own 1930s-era stamped-steel "tinplate" locomotives and cars in 1989, including this Standard Gauge 2-4-0.

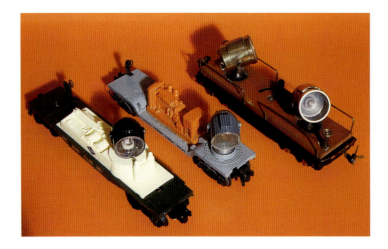

In the mid-1970s you could buy Lionel's Operating Searchlight Car as (left to right) a reproduction of the O Gauge flatcar, an O-27 Depressed Center Flatcar, and a Standard Gauge stamped-steel "tinplate" model.

Standard Gauge trains are, of course, proportionally larger than O Gauge trains. Lionel produced an entire range of Standard Gauge locomotives, cars, and accessories in the 1930s, as well as a similar line of O Gauge products. Most of these prewar products were stamped from steel that had been plated with tin to resist rusting. These stamped-steel products are referred to as "tinplate" among collectors.

In the early 1980s, Mike Wolf, operating under the name Mike's Train House (MTH), began selling exact replicas of Lionel's Standard Gauge and O Gauge "tinplate" toy trains from the 1930s. These reproductions were made in Korea.

In 1987, Lionel assumed the sales and marketing of this ever-growing line of Standard Gauge and O Gauge tinplate locomotives and cars, as well as reproductions of fabled accessories like Hell Gate Bridge. These Lionel replicas are so exact they have specific "new" dates stamped on them to avoid being sold as originals.

Lionel's first tinplate reproduction of a Standard Gauge locomotive was a black 2-4-2 steam engine with three red passenger cars. In 1989, Lionel introduced a gray 2-4-0 freight locomotive and four freight cars in Standard Gauge, as well as an O Gauge 4-4-2 *Hiawatha* streamliner with three articulated cars, and the 0-4-0 electric locomotive with four freight cars.

The massive "Lionel City" depot introduced in 1935, but listed as late as 1949 as the "Illuminated City Station," was reintroduced in 1988, and the smaller "Lionelville Station," with four dormers on its roof, was brought out again in 1989.

Lionel's Greatest Decade to Date
Lionel had something for just about everybody throughout the 1980s. You could, for example, buy brand-new re-creations of the 1930s Standard Gauge tinplate Floodlight Car, or pick your choice of either the O Gauge Depressed Center Floodlight Flatcar or conventional O Gauge floodlight flatcars first offered in the mid-1950s.

Lionel also produced some the least expensive models in their history during the 1980s, including some very short boxcars with molded-in doors that were used with sets that could be purchased by redeeming coupons from cereal

Lionel still offers boxcars in a variety of sizes, from authentically painted O Gauge cars (left) to the lower-cost O-27 cars (center) and stamped-steel reproductions of 1930s-era tinplate cars (right).

boxes. Similarly short cars with sliding doors were included in entry-level train sets at toy and chain stores. And Lionel continued to expand its series of O Gauge boxcars with dozens of railroad names never before seen on models, including cars that were part of the Famous American Railroad Series.

Lionel certainly did not ignore its heritage in the 1980s. In 1984, Lionel produced a completely new version of its famous 1937 "semi-scale" New York Central 4-6-4 Hudson steam locomotive. The exact-scale version of the 1937 Hudson would appear in 1990.

The 1984 model was massive; only the tender was slightly undersize and the boiler lacked some of the detail of the later "scale" version. The "scale" model's see-through spoked drivers, however, did appear as early as 1988 on the third variation of the semi-scale model, a gray version of the New York Central Hudson. This was the Hudson that was offered for direct sale in Boston & Albany lettering. The model included the most effective MagneTraction to date, with more magnets than the earlier steam locomotives, and it marked the beginning of Lionel products designed to appeal to both modelers and toy train enthusiasts.

In 1986, a matching O scale New York Central caboose was introduced along with a single-dome tank car with a platform around the dome. The "Standard O" boxcar had been introduced in 1973, but additional paint and lettering schemes were offered in the 1980s. All of these Standard O freight cars have trucks with real coil springs.

In the 1980s, Lionel also continued its series of "scale" extruded-aluminum passenger cars that had been introduced in 1979 with a brightly polished set of Burlington cars and with a red-and-orange Southern Pacific *Daylight* set in 1983. These passenger cars were of nearly correct O scale width and height but were shortened from a scale 86 feet to about 60 feet so they would look better on the relatively sharp curves.

In 1983, Fundimensions added smooth-side and smooth-roof passenger cars, beginning with a set of two-tone gray New York Central cars in 1983, a set of yellow-and-gray Union Pacific *Overland* cars in 1984, and, in 1985, a set of brown-and-orange Illinois Central *City of New Orleans* cars. The models all had interior lighting with silhouettes of the passengers on the windows similar to what Lionel offered in the postwar era on the much shorter plastic cars.

Lionel finally reintroduced the O-72 Wide Radius 65165 and 65166 switches in 1987. Prior to that, Lionel enthusiasts had been hoarding the O-72 switches that were last produced in 1942 to use with larger locomotives on larger layouts. These switches had 72-inch-circumference curved routes that would accept even the longest Lionel locomotive.

The 1980s marked the beginning of Lionel's recovery. The company had a new owner at the controls in Richard

Lionel reintroduced their most famous steam locomotive, the New York Central semi-scale Hudson, in 1984.

Kughn, a man who would see that the dreams of all Lionel enthusiasts would soon be realized. And it was just a beginning, for Lionel was about to grow both in size and in quality and introduce products in the next decade-plus that were not even dreamed of in Lionel's heyday in the 1950s. It was a great time to be a Lionel enthusiast.

CHAPTER 4
Lionel on Their Own Again

In this re-creation of the famous scene from the cover of the 1947 Lionel catalog, a full-scale Harriman 2-8-0 (in place of Pennsylvania Railroad 2-6-2) thunders past the Gateman's Shanty.

The Lionel 2-4-2 diesel was painted in "Lionel Steel" markings and sold in a set with two matching ore cars in 1996.

For Lionel, the 1990s were a period when dreams could finally become reality, thanks to the lower production and tooling costs of Korean and Chinese manufacturing facilities.

Lionel re-created itself during this period, with more new products and innovations than in any other period in its history. But it was also a period of growing nightmares for the company, as serious competition arrived from Mike's Train House (MTH) in 1990 and, later in the decade, from K-Line, as well as Atlas, Weaver, and Williams in the Hi-rail market.

Made in America in the 1990s

Lionel shifted the production of more common items like track and operating accessories to China in the early 1990s. Most of the new operating accessories and the larger locomotives were being made in China.

In their 1997 catalog, Lionel identified models that were made in America with small American flags, a step that effectively stressed what was *not* made in America more than it highlighted what *was*. The gradual shift to China, however, made it possible for Lionel to offer products at prices that the market would pay without totally losing their "Made in America" image.

Massive Models

The 1990s saw sweeping changes in three-rail trains, with dozens of locomotives and cars becoming available for true O scale. The popularity of "Hi-rail," which used exact-scale cars and locomotives on three-rail rather than two-rail track, really began to expand.

Lionel started the Hi-rail concept back in 1937 with their scale replica of the New York Central Class J1e 4-6-4 Hudson and their scale Pennsylvania Railroad Class B-6 0-6-0 switcher, and in 1940 with a true 1/48 scale boxcar, tank car, hopper, and caboose. These two locomotives and four freight cars were available with driver and wheel flanges to suit both the tubular-style, three-rail track and solid two-rail track.

Lionel created an all-new replica of the Hudson, complete with a scale-length tender for 1990. In the late 1980s, Lionel had offered a scale Hudson, but the tender was somewhat undersize; the 1990 version was accurate in every detail. Lionel followed up the Hudson with a series of scale locomotives that continues today.

Lionel's Alco RS-11 was introduced in D&H paint and lettering.

Lionel actually started this trend in 1989 with a full-scale model of the Reading Railroad's massive T-1 4-8-4 Northern and the Pennsylvania Railroad's Class B-6 0-6-0 switcher (a re-creation of the model Lionel had introduced in 1937). Lionel also introduced a full-scale 4-8-2 Mohawk in 1990, a full-scale version of their O-27 6-8-6 Pennsylvania S-2 turbine in 1991, and their first scale streamlined Dreyfuss Hudson and the three-truck Western Maryland Shay, both in 1992.

In 1999, Lionel introduced their first articulated steam locomotive, a replica of the Chesapeake & Ohio Railroad Allegheny 2-6-6-6 in both C&O and Virginian markings. The model is nearly exact O scale and is 32 inches long, as it should be! It weighs more than 17 pounds. Lionel closed out the twentieth century with the introduction of the largest locomotive ever made, an O scale replica of the Union Pacific 4-8-8-4 Big Boy articulated that was 32 inches long. The catalog invited buyers to "Enjoy the rumble!"

Smaller true O scale locomotives began to flow from Lionel in 1999 with the introduction of a 4-6-0 Camelback in Illinois Central, Pennsylvania, and Southern Pacific Railroad liveries. A Pennsylvania Railroad Pacific 4-6-2 lettered for the Pennsy, and a Pennsy Atlantic 4-4-2 lettered for the Pennsylvania, Baltimore & Ohio, and Santa Fe, both followed in 1999.

Lionel offered the first of a series of massive diesel locomotives in 1996, an O Gauge replica of the 12-wheeled General Electric Dash 9 diesel. The model was not full O scale, but it was more than 16 inches long. Lionel's first true O scale diesels, replicas of the EMD GP9 and GP20, were introduced in 1999. The true O scale GP20 is

The EMD SD40 was just one of the medium-size diesels that Lionel added to their O Gauge lineup in 1999.

In the 1990s, Lionel fans finally got the Alco PA-1 and PB-1 they had been requesting for five decades.

22-1/2 inches long, while Lionel's O Gauge version of the GP20 is just 14 inches long, illustrating that there really is a difference between O Gauge and Standard O locomotives. Lionel introduced O Gauge replicas of the massive EMD SD70 MAC and SD60 MAC locomotives in 1999, each 18 inches long. A 16-inch-long O Gauge replica of the EMD SD40 arrived in 1999.

Lionel enthusiasts had been begging for a Lionel version of the American Flyer Alco PA-1 diesel for 50 years and, in 1997, Lionel finally responded with a PA-1 painted in Santa Fe "warbonnet" colors. The PB-1 "B-unit" diesels came in 1998, along with a choice of Santa Fe, New York Central, and Erie PA-1 diesels. Pennsylvania Railroad PA-1 and PB-1 models arrived in 1999.

Full-Scale Freight Cars

Throughout the 1990s, Lionel expanded their series of true O scale freight cars beyond the 40-foot boxcar, plug-door reefer, gondola, and tank car introduced in the 1980s. Interestingly, Lionel does not always identify their true O scale locomotives as "exact scale." Lionel does, however, label their true O scale freight cars as "Standard O."

Lionel introduced a simulated-steel-side version of the O scale wood caboose and in the mid-1990s added an O scale replica of the ACF Centerflow two-bay covered hopper; a 100-ton, three-bay hopper; and a 50-foot, exterior-post, double-door boxcar. For comparison purposes, the O scale "50-foot" boxcar was 13-5/8 inches long, while the O Gauge modern-era (their previous boxcars having been

Lionel offers enough different railroad paint schemes to allow you to create your own one-road train.

In 1992, Lionel added a dome car to their series of extruded-aluminum, smooth-side passenger cars.

The new Lionel O Gauge steel-side caboose is a near-scale replica of the Santa Fe caboose that had been in Lionel's low-cost train sets since the 1940s.

based on real cars built in the 1940s and 1950s) 50-foot waffle-side boxcar was just 10-1/4 inches long. A true O scale boxcar would be 50 times 1/4 inches, or 12-1/2 inches plus the lengths of the couplers, so the new Lionel car was close enough to true O scale. A bulkhead flatcar, a standard flatcar, an articulated pair of intermodal cars with double-stack containers, a modern Unibody tank car, and a replica of the 12-wheeled Pennsylvania F9 depressed-center "well" car with two cable reels as load were all added in 1997. A three-bay ACF Centerflow covered hopper was added to the Lionel Standard O line in 1998. A bulkhead flatcar and a cylindrical covered hopper appeared in 1999.

The Operating Hopper Car introduced in 1957 came back in 2002 and was used with the reintroduced 456R Operating Coal Ramp.

Lionel's medium-size 4-6-2 Pacific-type steam locomotive offered in bright blue, orange, and ivory Lionel colors in 1999, became an instant "collector's item."

Lionel also expanded their line of O scale extruded-aluminum passenger cars, offering corrugated-side models in Santa Fe (1991 and 1996), Western Pacific *California Zephyr* (1993), and Katy *Texas Special* (1999) paint and lettering. Beginning with Great Northern in 1992, Lionel smooth-side offerings in O scale included Union Pacific, Norfolk & Western (1995), New York Central, Erie-Lackawanna (1994), and Milwaukee Road liveries.

Lionel also reintroduced modern plastic replicas of the famous Madison heavyweight Pullman cars, with three Pullmans and an observation car in Pennsylvania Railroad Tuscan Red with "Lionel Lines" on the letter boards, like the originals (1991), in Tuscan Red, lettered for Reading (1992), in red and orange Southern Pacific *Daylight* (1992), in Pullman Green (with "Pullman" on the letter boards), and in dark green (with "Jersey Central" on the letter boards).

Remote-Control Accessories

Lionel's production facilities in China allowed the company to finally reintroduce some of the accessories that were just too expensive to produce in America. Lionel started the 1990s with the introduction of a massive new Intermodal Crane that could pick up trailers from flatcars, move them beside the tracks, roll back and forth along the tracks, and deposit the trailers on the ground, just like real Mi-Jack cranes. It marked the beginning of a whole series of hands-off loading and unloading accessories, most reintroductions of postwar-era products.

These accessories add a special degree of realism to a Lionel layout because operators not only run the trains, they load and unload them. That means the trains aren't just running around but are actually carrying something the operator loaded—something that could later be unloaded.

In the last half of the decade, Lionel also brought back the yellow-and-green catalog No. 164 Log Loader from the 1946 to 1950 era that received logs on one track and carried them up a chain conveyor to dump them into waiting cars on a second track. Lionel also reintroduced the long Animated Sawmill that pushed logs in one end and "loaded" lumber out the other end. This sawmill, however, did not actually receive logs or load lumber.

The incredible stamped-steel 313 Bascule Bridge that hinged up to allow passing ships the right of way was reintroduced to re-create the original bridge from 1946 to 1949. The stamped-steel No. 497 Electric Coaling Station from 1946 to 1950 that received coal from one track, carried it up a chain conveyor in buckets, and dumped it into waiting cars reappeared in 1999.

The most incredible all-new accessories in Lionel's history began appearing in 1992, when Lionel introduced one of the most complex operating accessories to date: a three-piece Steam Clean & Wheel Grind Shop that simulated the wheel-grinding, train-washing, and steam-cleaning facilities of real railroads. Later in the decade, Lionel introduced the tinplate model of the Lionel Factory and the unbelievable Lionel Hobby Shop, with a full stock of Lionel items on its shelves and three operating layouts inside.

In 1998, Lionel rolled out a brand-new O Gauge switch to replace the Standard 031 switches that had been in production since the 1940s. The new 23010 (left) and 23011 (right) switches had short removable pieces of curved and straight track so they could be fitted into compact track plans. The switches worked especially well for freight yards with three or more parallel tracks because the tracks could be placed closer together. They also worked well with double-track mainlines for the same reason. Unfortunately, the curved portion was still the tight 31-inch circle of Standard O track, so they would not operate with all of the larger true O scale locomotives. For those massive models, Lionel continued to offer the Wide Radius 65165 and 65166 switches with 72-inch diameter curved routes.

Lionel introduced more inexpensive plastic kits in the 1990s, including this Operating Log Loader.

Lionel Collector Trains

Lionel has always been aware that there is a huge market for "collector" products. Each year, they introduce special O-27 and O Gauge locomotives and cars decorated for different states, football teams, Disney characters, and more. In addition, there is usually at least one Christmas-theme train in each Lionel catalog.

Recently, Lionel has used their classic orange, blue, and ivory paint scheme on collector cars and locomotives. In 1999, for example, Lionel offered a 44-ton diesel switcher and their classic 4-6-2 Pacific in the Lionel paint scheme.

Throughout the 1990s, Lionel certainly did not ignore the "toy" train market. The company continued production of O-27 steam and diesel locomotives and cars with new paint schemes each season. Lionel even expanded their plastic kit line to include a log loader and reintroduced the large Grain Elevator and Rico Station kits.

The massive Grain Elevator was one of series of plastic building kits offered by Lionel in the 1990s. The decals were not included.

Thomas the Tank Engine and Friends

Lionel had produced a Large Scale "Thomas the Tank" locomotive in 1989 and in 1998 introduced the O Gauge version of Thomas, along with replicas of the two passenger cars "Annie" and "Clarabel" in 1997 and the two "Troublesome Truck" gondolas in 1999. A depressed-center flatcar to carry "Harold the Helicopter" appeared in 1998, and the 0-4-0-T green "Percy" was offered in 1999.

50th Anniversary Dreams

Lionel did not ignore the O-27 segment of the market, for it was still (as it is now) their bread and butter. Lionel celebrated the 50th anniversary of their postwar line of products in 1994 by reintroducing a number of locomotives, cars, and accessories that had been hallmarks of the line.

One of the more memorable of these original postwar products was the 1950 Union Pacific streamlined train, headed with the 2023 Alco FA-1 and FB-1 pulling the all-new, smooth-sided streamlined passenger cars. In 1950, when Lionel illustrated their catalogs with paintings, not product photos, that Alco diesel and the train behind it looked just like the train one might see in real Union Pacific's Cheyenne, Wyoming, passenger terminal, for example.

In 1994, Lionel reintroduced near-exact replicas of the 1950 UP locomotives and cars, only the newer products had much-improved locomotive power and the cars carried "Union Pacific" lettering on the sides rather than the original's "Lionel Lines" markings.

The Lionel Century Club

In 1996, Lionel announced a series of five locomotives that would only be available to members of the new "Century Club." Production would be limited to the number of members, who had to sign up in advance if they wanted all five. The locomotives carried special numbers and gold-plated bells, and each came with its own wood base and Plexiglas display case.

The models included the 726 Berkshire 2-8-4, the small O-27 Pennsylvania Railroad 6-8-6 steam turbine, the Pennsylvania Railroad electric GG1, a pair of New York Central F3A diesels, and a 773 semi-scale New York Central 4-6-4 Hudson. This time, however, the models had to be ordered through a Lionel dealer, not directly from Lionel.

There was nothing particularly special about the locomotives beyond their guaranteed exclusivity, but it was certain acknowledgment of the collector value of Lionel products, even if they were reproductions and not originals. The program was not repeated.

More from Lionel's Tinplate Heritage

Lionel continued to expand their line of Lionel Classics, replicas from their own tinplate heritage. Lionel reproduced the massive Standard Gauge 4-4-4 steam locomotive and three passenger cars of the most famous pre–World War II set, the Standard Gauge 1929 *Blue Comet*, the Standard Gauge 4-4-4 *Fireball Express* with three cars in 1990, and, later, a replica of the "Old No. 7" 4-4-0 in polished brass with three yellow passenger cars with orange roofs.

Lionel introduced replicas of their O Gauge 1928 408E eight-wheeled electric locomotive with four passenger cars as the State Set, and a four-wheeled electric locomotive with four freight cars in Standard Gauge in 1991. In the early 1990s, Lionel also reproduced their tinplate O Gauge *Blue Comet* with a 2-4-2 steam locomotive, as well as replicas of their tinplate speedboats and 1912 slot car set.

In 1990, Lionel reintroduced a four-car articulated train similar to the Union Pacific M-10000 of 1935 but with a full head-end car like the 1936 *Hiawatha* set. Lionel also produced this same set of cars with the name "Rail Chief," like the 1937 Lionel set. This set of four articulated cars was cataloged to be pulled by the reintroduced Lionel full-size New York Central Hudson 4-6-4 steam locomotive, even though the cars themselves were lettered "Lionel Lines."

Lionel offered this 1/32 scale GP9 in several paint schemes in the 1990s as part of their Large Scale series that operated on two-rail track.

Lionel Large Scale

Lionel continued to produce Large Scale equipment to run on two-rail track with a 1-3/4-inch gauge. In 1990, Lionel introduced accurate 1/32 scale replicas of the EMD GP7, GP9, and GP20 diesels in 1/32 scale. But Lionel apparently expected its customers to look elsewhere for additional rolling stock. Additionally, Lionel continued to produce different road names for the Large Scale items that were introduced in the late 1980s.

American Flyer in the 1990s

There was enough demand for American Flyer locomotives, cars, and accessories for Lionel to continue its reintroduction of products in the 1990s. The EMD GP7 and the electric EP5 were introduced in 1991. The gorgeous Alco PA-1 was reintroduced as a PA-1/PA-1 pair with four passenger cars in Union Pacific colors as "American Railroad Series #8" in 1990, and a set of four silver Santa Fe passenger cars and a silver "warbonnet" pair of PA-1 diesels were introduced in 1997.

The American Flyer S scale PA-1 and PB-1 were reintroduced by Lionel in the 1990s after decades of being out of production.

In 1997, Lionel created two brand-new cars, an articulated pair of intermodal flatcars with trailers, and an extended-vision caboose.

The Sound of Steam (and Diesel Growl)

RailSounds appeared in 1990, carried in a second diesel locomotive or in a steam locomotive's tender. A speed trigger allowed three different rates of steam locomotive chuff or diesel growl. Both sounds were recordings of specific real locomotive sounds, as were the bell and whistle. RailSounds II was introduced in 1995 with digital recordings

The original Lionel "sound system" comprised an electric coil to simulate a diesel horn, a tiny bell, and a diaphragm that operated a whistle. The RailSounds are digitally recorded so they don't just sound real—they are real.

Run It like a Real Railroad

The advantage of a three-rail system like Lionel's is that there are no electrical gaps required at switches (turnouts), reverse loops, or wyes. Even with three-rail, however, there was still a need to divide the track into electrically isolated "blocks" in order to run two or more trains on the same track.

Lionel's version of the digital control command (DCC) used by HO scale-model railroaders needed to be somewhat more sophisticated than DCC for two reasons: Lionel uses AC rather than DC control, and the new Lionel system had to be compatible with any locomotive ever made by Lionel. This formidable task was met with the help of Lionel enthusiast, Lionel LLC shareholder, and recording artist Neil Young and a host of Lionel engineers and technicians. They called the Lionel system TrainMaster and it was introduced in 1995. It was Lionel's most significant accomplishment of the decade.

HO scale-model railroading, as a hobby, had evolved, by the mid-1990s, to provide individual control of several trains on the same track using DCC. DCC was available at a reasonable cost with many manufacturers offering plug-in installation and DCC-equipped locomotives.

It had been possible to operate two trains on the same track since the beginning of electric trains, but until the advent of DCC, this required electrically isolated "blocks" in the track with complex wiring and toggle switches to transfer control from one train's transformer and throttle to the second train's transformer and throttle. With DCC, the only electrical gaps needed were those to prevent short circuits at switches (turnouts) and for reverse loops or wyes. Lionel designed TrainMaster to offer all the

of specific real diesel locomotive sounds to match the model locomotive. Separate steam locomotive tenders and freight cars were made available with RailSounds II to provide realistic sounds for older Lionel models.

The more sophisticated sound chips were introduced in RailSounds 2.5 introduced in 1998, which was mounted in acoustically sealed chambers in the diesel or in the steam locomotive tender to enhance the quality of the sound. RailSounds 4.0 added a more powerful amplifier and, for steam locomotives, a variable "DynaChuff" sound that would increase in volume as the speed increased.

advantages of DCC but with a simpler system that requires just one command base for the entire layout.

With the conventional block control systems it is necessary for the engineer to pay more attention to turning the blocks on and off than to actually running his or her train. With DCC systems, the operator can run a train the way a real engineer would, watching for other trains, for correctly routed switches, and for signals that indicate other trains ahead. With TrainMaster, the operator also has the option of controlling all the switches and signals from a single handheld keypad.

In fact, with TrainMaster, it's possible to run two trains, setting one on "automatic" while focusing attention on the other. It is also possible to "park" up to 100 locomotives, with each available at the touch of a button on the keypad. In essence, with TrainMaster the operator controls the train, not the model railroad—and the realism is breathtaking.

The TrainMaster System

TrainMaster is designed to be the ultimate in model train control. First, the operator no longer needs to sit beside a transformer, working the buttons—control is in a handheld keypad. That keypad has a wireless connection to the TrainMaster command base, allowing the operator to walk around the track alongside the locomotive or to sit back in an easy chair and watch it run. The operator can adjust the speeds of up to 100 locomotives, throw switches to send the trains on alternate routes, operate coupling and uncoupling, and activate accessories like log loaders, coal loaders, coal and log dumpers, milk depots, mail stations, and the host of other Lionel action cars and industries.

It's even possible to control signals and turn lights on or off in buildings, beside streets, and in towers. And, oh yes, TrainMaster also allows the operator to control the sound of any TrainMaster-equipped steam or diesel locomotive; actuate the horns, whistle, and bell; activate crew commands through CrewTalk, and hear the tower's orders through TowerTalk. Furthermore, TrainMaster does not interfere with the automatic actuation of highway crossing guards, gates and flashers, or block signals and semaphores that Lionel had already established. The system also operates with any Lionel locomotive ever made. And all of this is controlled from a handheld keypad the size of television remote control.

The TrainMaster system is not magic—it's a clever adaptation of today's digital microprocessors to fulfill the dreams of model railroaders. The TrainMaster system features five basic components: 1) a conventional Lionel transformer to provide the basic low-voltage AC current; 2) a PowerMaster or Track Power Controller module to convert the AC to the needs of the new system; 3) a Command Base to receive the signals and send them through the tracks to the locomotives, couplers, switches, and accessories; 4) a CAB-1 Remote Control handheld keypad with a throttle control knob; and 5) a locomotive equipped with TrainMaster digital receiver. Actually, the system will run one conventional locomotive even if it does not have a receiver; the receivers become necessary when you want to run two or more locomotives. If you have an older Lionel layout that you have already wired into blocks, Lionel offers the Block Power Controller to turn the blocks on and off via the keypad.

The TrainMaster system is simple to use—just connect the wires between the five components; hook up the transformer, PowerMaster (or Track Power Controller), Command Base, and the track; put the locomotive on the rails; grab the CAB-1 Remote Controller; and run the train. If you want to run two trains at once, both need to be equipped with TrainMaster receivers. Most newer Lionel locomotives have this feature, but you also have the option of purchasing already-wired tenders for steam locomotives or receivers that can be installed in some Lionel locomotives by an authorized Lionel serviceperson.

Lionel's greatest achievement in train control is the TrainMaster system offering the option of remotely controlling up to 100 trains with a handheld keypad. The locomotive here is an SD90 MAC from the 2000 lineup.

Real Loads for Locomotives

The Lionel TrainMaster system's most exciting advantage, to many model railroaders, is that it offers adjustable speed and braking controls. You can adjust the momentum of the locomotive so it takes about as long for the model to get started, even when cranked at full throttle, as it does for a real locomotive to get started. If that's not slow enough, crank in even more momentum and you can simulate the effort a real locomotive makes when getting a full train started, with the locomotive moving forward slowly enough to take up the slack in the train one coupler at a time.

Similarly, braking can be adjusted so the train takes dozens of feet to slow to a stop, just like a real train. There's also an emergency stop feature on the Lionel system that's not on the real locomotive's braking system so you can stop it sooner if you miscalculate how much track you needed to bring the loaded train to a halt. Both the slow start and slow stop functions are adjustable from the handheld keypad.

Lionel began using their new Odyssey nine-pole motors in the larger locomotives in 1998. The motor has more than twice the power of the older Lionel motor while reducing power consumption. No oiling is needed with the sealed bearings. Even with conventional control, Odyssey-equipped locomotives start more smoothly and respond more directly to throttle control than do models equipped with older motors.

Hands-Off Uncoupling Anywhere

The Lionel ElectroCouplers, when used with the TrainMaster system, allow you to uncouple locomotives and rolling stock anywhere on the track. There is no need to stop directly over one of the Lionel Remote-Control Track sections to actuate the couplers.

Many Lionel locomotives today are equipped with ElectroCouplers and a few of the larger freight cars also include them. Lionel also offers replacement trucks with ElectroCouplers for freight cars so you can retrofit them to as many cars as you wish. RailSounds even re-creates the clanking sound of the couplers!

In some ways, Lionel is still the Lionel of the 1940s and 1950s, with a slate of fascinating O-27 and O Gauge toy trains. Lionel is also, however, Hi-rail models in massive exact 1/48 scale. And both types can be run on the same track, up to 100 at a time with uncoupling, loading, dumping, and route changing all controlled from the TrainMaster handheld keypad. You can hear the sounds of real railroading and, best of all, you can actually feel the rumble as the massive Lionel models roll down the track.

The EMD F3A and F3B have been Lionel's most popular diesel since their introduction in the 1950s.

The exact-scale Santa Fe articulated 2-8-8-2 locomotive has all the handrails, pipes, and other details of its prototype.

CHAPTER 5
The Lionel Dream Fulfilled

Lionel's future is pretty clear. Lionel will continue to manufacture reproductions of the toy trains of the 1950s and earlier, often with exciting new paint schemes.

The real growth of the hobby, and the direction Lionel seems to be taking, however, is rooted in three areas: 1) Hi-rail trains built to exact 1/48 scale to operate on three-rail track; 2) control systems for all types of Lionel trains that allow operation of several locomotives at the same time, as well as coupling, uncoupling, switching, and accessory operations accessories from a handheld keypad; and 3) the creation of truly fantastic operating accessories, such as complete locomotive shops and carnivals, all in massive O scale. In other words, it's more of the same products that Lionel produced during the first few years of this new millennium.

The major change for Lionel in the new century has been the shift of all production to China. Lionel had been making track in China since the 1980s and the new operating accessories were produced in China beginning in the mid-1990s. In 2000, however, Lionel closed it manufacturing plant in Mount Clemens, Michigan, and shifted all production to China. Only the design and marketing forces remain in a new Detroit area office.

Collecting Lionel

Although not every Lionel enthusiast has a layout, every Lionel enthusiast *is* a collector. Lionel locomotives and rolling stock, therefore, comprise the most important part of the Lionel line and the company is doing everything it can imagine to make those products more interesting each year. Lionel continues to produce entry-level O-27 train sets and individual locomotives and cars. Lionel is also making that tradition visible with "collector" paint schemes on even their Large Scale locomotives. The looks change each year, which makes the products interesting to collectors as well as to newcomers to the hobby.

The massive 4-6-6-4 Challenger is an articulated steam locomotive on which each set of drivers pivots beneath the boiler.

LEFT: The New York Central 4-6-4 Hudson with streamlined shrouding created by industrial designer Henry Dreyfuss.

In 2000, Lionel introduced their first all-new O-27 entry-level diesel in decades, a small-size version of the EMD FTA and FTB diesels that are priced low enough to be included in the better sets. Lionel also offered the massive SD90 MAC diesel with all the real railroad paint schemes you would expect, but they offered it with the orange, blue, and ivory Lionel colors. Lionel has also discovered that enthusiasts want more steam locomotives, so they add two or three to the line each year. Because all of these products are offered in limited supplies, each is a collector piece in addition to having value for those who, say, are modeling the Union Pacific and want everything Lionel makes in UP. And the performance of even the entry-level locomotives far exceeds that of any equivalent Lionel locomotive of the past.

TrainMaster Matures

Advances in electronics have made it possible for the Lionel TrainMaster system to perform even more tasks than were possible with the earlier systems. In the beginning, Train-Master only operated locomotives equipped with the TrainMaster receivers. Today, TrainMaster operates almost any toy train locomotive that will run on Lionel track and allows complete control over the entire range of RailSounds.

TrainMaster controls can be adjusted so the locomotive really does "feel" like it has a 100-car train of 100-ton cars taxing the power capacity of the locomotive. The laborious, almost imperceptible, start of the train can be duplicated with complete control from that handheld keypad so the slack between each coupler of each car in the train is taken up one car at a time—again, just like the real trains.

Lionel has improved the TrainMaster system to provide more effective digital microprocessors in the locomotives for smoother throttle response. The newer units are small enough that they can fit even in a switcher.

Lionel is also making it easier to get started with TrainMaster by providing low-cost locomotives like the GP7 equipped with Command Control receivers and RailSounds. Lionel locomotives equipped with the Odyssey System have automatic speed control that maintains the speed regardless of up- or downhill grades. Lionel labeled the motors that have been used since the late 1990s "Odyssey," but the "Odyssey System" is an electronic control separate from the motor itself.

Lionel has continued to improve the TrainMaster system, offering a host of controllers to allow digital control of the conventional block systems, to provide for operations of operating accessories like log and coal loaders, to control track uncoupling and load-dumping or unloading sections, and to control switches. Lionel now offers an Action Recorder Controller that allows the operator to program a sequence of commands.

The Action Recorder Controller has up to eight memory functions that would allow you, for example, to stop the train, uncouple the locomotive from a loaded coal car, turn the switch from mainline to siding, switch the loaded car into the siding, uncouple from the car, head back out of the siding, turn the switch back to the mainline, and recouple to the train—all without touching a button. Alternately, the system would also allow you to run a train into an alternate track route on one lap and back onto the original route on the next without touching a button.

Lionel has also increased the number of PowerMaster alternatives with two Track Power Controllers that offer up to 400 watts of power and a wider choice of transformers.

Real Sounds from RailSounds

Lionel has improved the RailSounds system to include specific real diesel engine sounds unique to each brand of locomotive so that an Alco sounds different from a GE, which sounds different from an EMD diesel, just like the prototypes. There's also a startup sound that duplicates the sound of a

Lionel's most realistic diesel locomotive to date, the 2003 exact-scale replica of the Santa Fe F3A diesel, comes complete with marker flags and other "superdetails."

Lionel reintroduced the 1950s O-27 Auto Rack Car in several paint schemes, including this 2002 reproduction of the original.

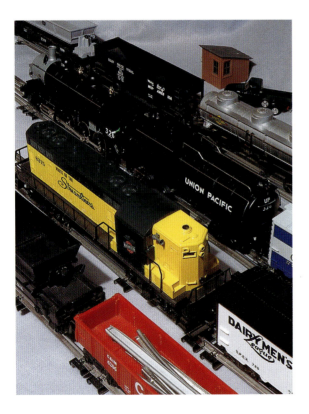

steam locomotive firing up or a diesel engine starting when you turn on the system power. The speed and intensity of the diesel or steam exhaust also increases, of course, as the speed of the train increases.

When RailSounds is actuated by Lionel's TrainMaster command control, additional sound-effect options include brakes, blowing off steam from the cylinders of steam locomotive, and even the clanking of operating couplers. There is also a set of three different recorded voices that duplicate the words that are heard when real trains are

The Harriman 2-8-0 will operate alongside the EMD GP9 and, with TrainMaster Command Control, the two can run at the same time.

operated, including TowerCom Announcements from the control tower that call out the locomotive's number or road name to be "clear for departure." CrewTalk Communication duplicates the orders the crew communicates to the engineer or to the crew in the caboose. StationSounds is housed in some Lionel passenger cars to provide the sounds of the station and reports from the conductor.

Modern Re-creations from China

Lionel has been producing replicas of the locomotives, cars, and accessories from their 1945 to 1960 postwar heyday for the past three decades. These products utilize the original tooling for most of the visible parts of the products with the added bonus of modern mechanisms. Now, Lionel also produces replicas of their own products from the more recent 1970–2000 period with extra details made possible by the lower production costs in China.

Lionel turned the move to China into an opportunity both to maintain prices at a competitive level and to offer a better product for the price. Take, for example, the *Overland Limited* set of 15-inch-long (about 60 feet in O scale) extruded-aluminum Union Pacific yellow and gray streamlined passenger cars that were first introduced in 1984. The 2002 *Overland Limited* set was made in China and includes replicas of the 1984 baggage cars, coaches, and observation cars (but no combine).

Lionel introduced the Harriman 2-8-0 Consolidation in 2000 in a choice of Union Pacific or Southern Pacific markings.

Lionel's new-for-2002 extruded-aluminum passenger cars have full interiors, including passengers. The drumheads on the observation cars are illuminated, as are the interiors.

In 2003, an additional coach and diner were made available. Unlike the 1984 products, however, the cars that are made in China have full interiors with seats and walls and even painted passengers and lighting that beams down from the ceiling of the cars. The 1984 cars that were made in Mount Clemens had silhouettes of the passengers on the windows and a few lightbulbs at about window level. These more recent cars look like the paintings that illustrated the 1950 Lionel catalog that was the "wish book" of many a baby boomer, but they are also just long enough to look great on curves as tight as 42 inches.

The new cars make the dome cars that Lionel introduced in 1992 look a bit toylike, but they all match closely enough, for example, to make a dream-fulfilling Union Pacific streamliner like that prototype I saw in Cheyenne, Wyoming, as a child. Lionel has also continued to produce and expand this series of extruded-aluminum corrugated and smooth-side streamlined passenger cars.

In the new century, Lionel produced even more of these extruded-aluminum passenger cars with corrugated sides for the Rio Grande (*California Zephyr*), Pennsylvania, Canadian Pacific, Southern, MKT (*Texas Special*), Delaware

Lionel's Amtrak *Superliner* cars are the longest passenger cars Lionel has made to date. Like the 2002 extruded-aluminum passenger cars, they have full interiors and lighting.

In 2002, Lionel created an O scale replica of the General Electric Dash 8-32BWH used by Amtrak.

The Lionel U30C features TrainMaster, RailSounds, ElectroCouplers, and Odyssey System control in a near-scale replica.

& Hudson, Santa Fe, Rio Grande, and Lionel Lines. Lionel also offered extruded smooth-side cars for New York Central, Norfolk & Western, Pennsylvania, Northern Pacific, Kansas City Southern, and Erie-Lackawanna, in addition to more Union Pacific cars.

In 2001, Lionel also introduced a near-scale Amtrak *Superliner* car that is 18 inches long, just a few inches short of being exact scale. A new series of Madison-style heavyweight passenger cars was also introduced for the new century. The new cars are 19-1/2 inches long, which is 78 feet long in O scale and about 6 feet short of exact scale. An exact-scale 86-foot passenger car would be about 21-1/2 inches long, longer than Lionel's largest diesels.

The new "heavyweights" have flexible diaphragms to fill the space between the cars, a first for Lionel that greatly enhances their realism. A Pullman, observation car, baggage car, and combine are available.

Lionel's 4-6-6-4 Challenger is a full-scale model, but it can negotiate 31-inch curves.

Massive Motive Power

For those with limited space, Lionel still offers the traditional O-27 line of small steam and diesel locomotives, short freight cars, and short passenger cars. For those Lionel fans who love Lionel for the sheer mass that O scale offers, Lionel produces some really huge replicas of some really huge real locomotives.

The EMD F3A and F3B diesels have been symbols of Lionel since they were introduced in the 1948 catalog. In 2003, Lionel produced the first F3A and F3B models in exact O scale. The new diesels have wire handrails; etched-metal, see-through grilles; full interiors; and, of course, TrainMaster and RailSounds. The real locomotives feature brackets to hold flags that indicate the train is a lone train or if there is another section following. On the 2003 Lionel F3A, these marker flags are miniature American flags.

Lionel introduced its replica of General Electric's largest diesel, the Dash 9, in the 1990s and they continue

The Santa Fe 2-8-8-2 articulated is another replica of real steam locomotive in exact 1/48 scale.

to offer the locomotive in a new paint scheme each year. In 2000, Lionel produced their replica of EMD's massive SD90 MAC, SD80 MAC, a new SD70 MAC, and the SD40-2. They also rolled out the General Electric 16-wheeled Union Pacific gas turbine "Verandah" locomotive; the GE U33C, U30C, and U28CG "U-boats"; and a GE Dash 8-32BWH.

The medium-size locomotives that are Lionel's tradition have also been improved with new models in the twenty-first century, including a replica of the Alco S-2 and S-4 switchers, Alco C-420, EMD GP30, Fairbanks-Morse H16-44, EMD E6A passenger diesels, and new near-scale Alco FA-2 and FB-2 diesels.

The series of medium-size O scale steam locomotives has been expanded to include a USRA 0-8-0 Switcher, USRA 4-6-2 Pacific, USRA 4-8-2 Mountain, a Pennsylvania Railroad H-9 2-8-0 Consolidation and Class K-4 4-6-2, a Harriman 2-8-0 Consolidation and Harriman 4-4-2 Atlantic, a 4-6-0 Ten-Wheeler, and the New York Central 4-6-4.

Lionel's series of articulated steam locomotives also continues to grow with the introduction, in the new millennium, of the Pennsylvania Railroad's 4-4-4-4 class T-1 Duplex; the Norfolk & Western 2-8-8-4 Class A; the Challenger 4-6-6-4 in Union Pacific, Western Maryland, Clinchfield, and Rio Grande lettering; USRA 2-6-6-2; and Union Pacific and Santa Fe 2-8-8-2s. These massive locomotives have been engineered to negotiate Lionel curves as sharp as 54 inches. (The 4-6-6-4s will actually negotiate 31-inch curves, but look a bit odd doing so.)

ABOVE: Lionel introduced this new O scale operating coal dump car in 2002.

LEFT: The 364 Conveyor Lumber Loader reproduction has the stamped-steel construction of the original 1948 version.

BOTTOM: The 397 Coal Loader is back after a half-century absence from the Lionel line.

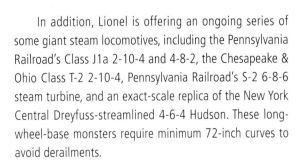

In addition, Lionel is offering an ongoing series of some giant steam locomotives, including the Pennsylvania Railroad's Class J1a 2-10-4 and 4-8-2, the Chesapeake & Ohio Class T-2 2-10-4, Pennsylvania Railroad's S-2 6-8-6 steam turbine, and an exact-scale replica of the New York Central Dreyfuss-streamlined 4-6-4 Hudson. These long-wheel-base monsters require minimum 72-inch curves to avoid derailments.

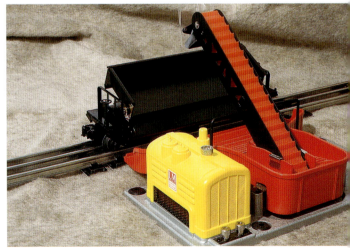

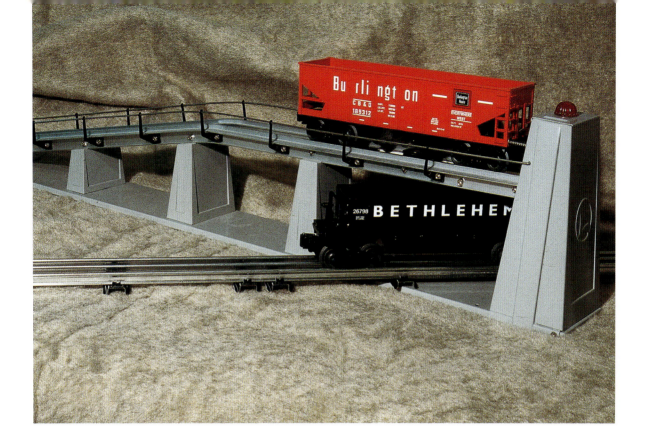

Lionel reproduced the 456 Operating Coal Ramp that automatically uncouples the car from the train and opens the hopper doors. It can be used with the 397 Coal Loader or a track can be placed beneath it (as shown) to dump "coal" right into waiting hoppers.

The newest Lionel steam locomotives have a wireless connection between the tender and the locomotive so all you need to do is connect the drop-in drawbar; there's no more need to plug and unplug and no wires to break between the locomotive and tender.

Standard O Freight Cars

Lionel has also added new tooling to their line of exact-scale Standard O freight cars with a 50-foot single-door, exterior-post boxcar; 40-foot PS-1 boxcars with 8-foot and 6-foot doors; Pullman-Standard PS-2 4427 three-bay covered hoppers; 52-foot, 6-inch-long PS-5 gondolas; 50-foot PS-4 flatcars; and GATX Tank Train tank cars. Then there are all-new scale-detailed tooling to the bay-window caboose and extended-vision caboose with details to match other "scale" cars.

Operating Accessories

Lionel has now produced re-creations of every remote-controlled accessory from the postwar era. Some of the original tooling has been moved to China, but most of these replicas of earlier operating accessories are made

Lionel has reproduced all of their exciting remote-control accessories from the 1950s, including the stamped-steel 97 Coal Elevator (left) with chain-hoisted buckets, and the 497 Coaling Station with cable-hoisted bin.

from new dies that match the shape of the originals, yet provide improved operation.

In the twenty-first century, Lionel has already produced re-creations of the 364 Conveyor Lumber Loader and the 397 Diesel Operating Coal Loader from the 1948 catalog, the 456 Coal Ramp from the 1950 catalog, the 497 Coaling Station with cable-operated lift bin from the 1953 catalog, and the 362 Barrel Loader from the 1954 catalog.

Lionel is also constantly inventing new operating accessories like the Operating Fork Lift platform that loads stacks of lumber onto waiting flatcars. The Rotary Coal Tipple duplicates the action of coal unloaders at power plants where the entire car is rotated 360 degrees to dump its load into a bin. When used with the 397 Coal Loader, the cars can be reloaded to begin the cycle all over again in the tradition of Lionel's classic coal and log loaders. And, the company offers an operating set of carnival accessories, including a 20-inch-tall Ferris wheel, a carousel, and a Pirate Ship Ride.

Lionel Tinplate Classics
While Lionel still produces replicas of its tinplate Standard Gauge and O Gauge locomotives and cars from the 1930s, the company has also added new products designed to

Most Lionel locomotives today feature MagneTraction or plastic traction tires so they can climb steep grades on multilevel layouts like this one.

capture the tinplate look, including a Standard Gauge Milwaukee Road *Hiawatha*, a red, orange, and gray streamlined 4-6-4 steam locomotive with, for the first time, TrainMaster and RailSounds. There's even a four-car set of tinplate passenger cars to match. In 2001, Lionel offered a Standard Gauge tinplate replica of the New York Central *Commodore Vanderbilt* 4-6-4 with three matching tinplate coaches.

Lionel Large Scale

Lionel produces the Large Scale 0-6-0T, four-wheeled caboose and eight-wheeled gondola in a variety of Christmas-theme paint in the new century. In addition, the Large Scale "Thomas the Tank Engine" is back in the Lionel lineup with the coaches "Annie" and "Clarabel."

American Flyer from Lionel

Lionel continues to make replicas of American Flyer S scale locomotives, rolling stock, and accessories.

In 2002, Lionel introduced the largest operating accessory American Flyer ever produced, the Seaboard Coaler. American Flyer made the loader in 1947 and it is one of the most spectacular of all the operating accessories sold by Lionel. The clamshell bucket picks up coal, which is then moved in toward the tower and up by small trolley and track. The coal is then dumped into the black bin inside the tower where it can be loaded, via a chute, with a remote-controlled gate, into a waiting hopper or gondola.

Lionel's Second 100 Years

All of the products that Lionel produces today are better than the products Lionel produced in its heyday, the 1950s. After decades of struggling, Lionel finally was forced by its competition to move production to China. Without that move, there would be no Lionel.

Lionel has taken every opportunity that production in China offers to improve their products while still keeping the original designs that have so delighted Lionel fans over the years. It is quite clear from the products Lionel has introduced since the move to China that they intend to fulfill those dreams of the children of the 1940s, 1950s, and 1960s, as well as the dreams of today's children, however old they may be. Each new catalog brings more surprises than at other any time in Lionel's history. For Lionel fans, this is the best period in the company's history.

The American Flyer Seaboard Loader is now available as brand-new reproduction with the same operating excitement of the original.

INDEX

Accessories, 28, 31, 37, 38, 40, 42, 44, 48, 49, 59, 60, 61, 63, 77, 78, 80–82, 84, 88, 89
    97 Coal Elevator, 90
    164 Log Loader, 64
    282 Gantry Crane, 44
    313 Bascule Bridge, 63
    352 Animated Ice Depot, 44
    362 Barrel Loader, 90
    364 Conveyor Lumber Loader, 88, 90
    397 Coal Loader, 88–90
    464 Lumber Mill, 44
    456R Operating Coal Ramp, 61, 89
    497 Electric Coaling Station, 63, 90
    Animated sawmill, 63
    Carnival, 90
    Freight platform, 23
    Freight station, 22, 23, 45
    Gateman's shanty, 9, 23, 27, 52, 53
    Grain elevator, 64, 65
    Illuminated City Station, 48
    Lionel City, 48
    Lionel Factory, 63
    Lionel Hobby Shop, 63
    Lionelville Station, 48
    Magnetic crane, 42, 44
    Oil drum loader, 38
    Operating fork lift platform, 90
    Rail Chief, 66
    Rico station, 45, 64
    Rotary coal tipple duplicate, 90
    Seaboard coaler, 38
    Seaboard loader, 92, 93
    Steam Clean & Wheel Grind Shop, 63
American Flyer, 13, 14, 37, 38, 67, 68, 93
Aristo-Craft, 40
Atlas, 17, 54
Bachmann, 40
Century Club, 66
Cohen, Joshua Lionel, 35
Collector Series, 37
CrewTalk, 70
DCC (Digital Control Command), 69, 70
ElectroCouplers, 73
Famous American Railroad Series, 37, 43, 44, 45, 49
Gauges,
    Definition, 12, 13
    HO, 7, 20, 35, 44, 69
    Large Scale (G scale), 14, 15, 35, 38–40, 42, 44, 66, 67, 77, 93
    O, 8, 12, 16, 35, 37, 38, 40, 44, 45, 47, 48, 57–59, 63, 64, 66, 73, 83, 85, 87, 90
    O-27, 7, 8, 12, 13, 16, 31, 45, 64, 66, 73, 77, 78, 85
    O-72, 50, 63
    N, 35
    S, 13, 14, 35, 68
    Standard O (Standard), 8, 12–16, 35, 38, 39, 46–48, 58, 66, 89, 90, 93
General Mills, 20, 35
    MPC, 20
    Fundimensions ("A Division of General Mills Fun Group, Inc."), 20, 23, 34, 45, 50
Handbook for Model Builders, The, 37
Hi-rail, 14, 15, 54, 55, 77
Johnson, Ralph, 17, 20, 21, 31
K-Line, 17, 54
Kughn, Richard, 34, 35, 38, 50, 51
Lionel's 50th anniversary, 66
Lionel's 75th anniversary, 28
Lionel Train Book, The, 37
LGB, 39, 40
MagneTraction, 49, 91
Models,
    0-4-0T, 27, 28, 44
    6-8-6 steam turbine, 66
    726 Berkshire, 44
    Alco C-420, 87
    Alco FA-1 (O-27), 13, 28, 66
    Alco FA-2, 87
    Alco FB-1, 66
    Alco FB-2, 87
    Alco PA-1, 58, 67, 68, 69
    Alco PB-1, 58, 68, 69
    Alco RS-11, 55
    Alco RS3 (O-27), 13, 28
    Allegheny, 57
    Atlantic, 40, 57
    Big Boy, 57
    Blue Comet, 66
    California Zephyr, 63, 82
    Camelback, 57
    Challenger, 77, 85, 88
    City of New Orleans, 50
    Class A, 8

Class B-6, 55, 57
Class J1a, 88
Class S-2 turbine, 44, 45, 57
Class T-1, 88
Class T-2, 88
Commodore Vanderbilt, 93
Congressional Limited, 27
Dash 8-32BWH, 86
Dash 9, 57, 83, 85
Daylight, 63
E-33, 28
EP5 "Little Joe", 25, 28, 67
F3A, 8, 17, 21, 44, 72, 73, 79, 85
F3B, 8, 21, 44, 72, 73, 85
FA2, 44, 66
Fairbanks-Morse H16-44, 87
Fairbanks-Morse TrainMaster, 40, 41, 44
FB-1, 17
FB-1, 17
Fireball Express, 66
FT (EMD), 13, 78
General, 13, 35
GG1, 28, 66
GP7, 13, 18, 25, 28, 40, 67, 78
GP9, 25, 28, 37, 40, 44, 57, 67, 80
GP20, 57, 67
GP30, 87
H-9, 87
Harriman, 6, 52, 53, 80, 81
Hiawatha, 48, 93
Madison series, 13, 28, 29, 37, 63, 84
Mohawk, 57
New York Central Hudson series, 10, 11, 27, 28, 38, 44, 49–51, 55, 66, 76, 77, 88
NW2, 26–28, 31
"Old No. 7", 66
Overland Limited, 50, 81
Reading Railroad T-1, 44, 57
SD40 (EMD), 56, 57
SD40-2, 86
SD60 MAC, 58
SD70 MAC, 58, 86
SD80 MAC, 86
SD90 MAC, 71, 78, 86
Superliner, 83, 84
Texas Special, 21, 63, 82
U28CG, 86

U30C, 84, 86
U33C, 86
U36B, 25
USRA, 87
"Verandah", 86
MTH (Mike's Train House) 17, 48, 54
Odyssey nine-pole motors, 73, 78
Odyssey System, 78, 84
Pola, 45
Radioscope, 42, 44
RailSounds, 68, 69, 73, 78, 80, 84
RailSounds II, 69
Rolling stock,
    Extruded-aluminum passenger cars, 82, 83
    GATX Tank Train tank cars, 89
    Milk car, 30, 44
    O gauge flatcar, 48
    O-27 Auto rack car, 80
    O-27 Depressed center flatcar, 48
    Operating boxcar, 30, 48
    Operating coal dump car, 88
    Operating hopper car, 61
    Passenger cars, 33, 60, 82
    Passenger station, 22, 23, 45
    PS-1 boxcar, 89
    PS-2 4427 three-bay covered hopper, 89
    PS-4 flatcar, 89
    PS-5 gondola, 89
    Searchlight car, 22, 31, 48
    Standard O freight car, 89
    Steel-side caboose, 60
Thomas & Friends, 42
Thomas the Tank Engine, 39, 42, 66, 93
    Annie, 66, 93
    Clarabel, 66, 93
    Harold the Helicopter, 66
    Percy, 66
    Troublesome Truck gondolas, 66
Tinplate, 14, 46–48, 66, 90, 93
TowerTalk, 70
TrainMaster, 69–71, 73, 77, 80, 84
USA Trains, 40
Weaver, 17, 54
Williams, 17, 54
Wolf, Mike, 48
Young, Neil, 69

Other MBI Publishing Company titles of interest:

Hot Wheels Cars
ISBN: 0-7603-0839-X

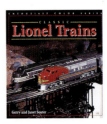
Classic Lionel Trains
ISBN 0-7603-1138-2

Classic Toy Trains
ISBN: 0-7603-1367-9

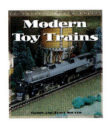
Modern Toy Trains
ISBN 0-7603-1179-X

Matchbox Cars
ISBN 0-7603-0964-7

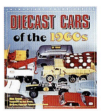
Diecast Cars of the 1960s
ISBN: 0-7603-0719-9

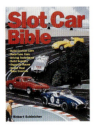
Slot Car Bible
ISBN 0-7603-1153-6

101 Projects for Your Model Railroad
ISBN 0-7603-1181-1

Big Book of Model Railroad Track Plans
ISBN 0-7603-1423-3

Find us on the Internet at www.motorbooks.com 1-800-826-6600